CERBERUS,
THE DOG OF HADES

CERBERUS,
THE DOG OF HADES

MAURICE BLOOMFIELD

ISBN: 978-93-5614-675-4

Published: 1905

© 2022
LECTOR HOUSE LLP

LECTOR HOUSE LLP
E-MAIL: info@lectorhouse.com

EXPLANATION OF FRONTISPIECE

The picture is reproduced from Baumeister's *Denkmäler des klassichen Alterthums*, volume I., figure 730 (text on p. 663). It is on a vase and describes one of the twelve heroic deeds of Herakles. The latter, holding aloft his club, drags two-headed Cerberus out of Hades by a chain drawn through the jaw of one of his heads. He is just about to pass Cerberus through a portal indicated by an Ionic pillar. To the right Persephone, stepping out of her palace, seems to forbid the rape. Herakles in his turn seems to threaten the goddess, while Hermes, to the left, holds a protecting or restraining arm over him. Athene, with averted face, ready to depart with her protégé, stands in front of four horses hitched to her chariot. Upon her shield the eagle augurs the success of the entire undertaking.

CERBERUS, THE DOG OF HADES
THE HISTORY OF AN IDEA

BY

MAURICE BLOOMFIELD

Professor of Sanskrit and Comparative Philology
Johns Hopkins University

1905

**To the Memory
of
F. Max Müller**

CONTENTS

CERBERUS,
THE DOG OF HADES

Hermes, the guide of the dead, brings to Pluto's kingdom their psyches, "that gibber like bats, as they fare down the dank ways, past the streams of Okeanos, past the gates of the sun and the land of dreams, to the meadow of asphodel in the dark realm of Hades, where dwell the souls, the phantoms of men outworn." So begins the twenty-fourth book of the *Odyssey*. Later poets have Charon, a grim boatsman, receive the dead at the River of Woe; he ferries them across, provided the passage money has been placed in their mouths, and their bodies have been duly buried in the world above. Otherwise they are left to gibber on the hither bank. Pluto's house, wide-gated, thronged with guests, has a janitor Kerberos, sometimes friendly, sometimes snarling when new guests arrive, but always hostile to those who would depart. Honey cakes are provided for them that are about to go to Hades—the sop to Cerberus. This dog, nameless and undescribed, Homer mentions simply as the dog of Hades, whom Herakles, as the last and chief test of his strength, snatched from the horrible house of Hades.[1] First Hesiod and next Stesichorus discover his name to be Kerberos. The latter seems to have composed a poem on the dog. Hesiod[2] mentions not only the name but also the genealogy of Kerberos. Of Typhaon and Echidna he was born, the irresistible and ineffable flesh-devourer, the voracious, brazen-voiced, fifty-headed dog of hell.

Plato in the *Republic* refers to the composite nature of Kerberos.[3] Not until Apollodorus (2. 5. 12. 1. ff.), in the second century B. C., comes the familiar description: Kerberos now has three dog heads, a dragon tail, and his back is covered with the heads of serpents. But his plural heads must have been familiarly assumed by the Greeks; this will appear from the evidence of their sculptures and vase-paintings.

---

[1] *Iliad* viii. 368; *Odyssey* xi. 623.

[2] *Theogony*, 311 ff.; cf. also 769 ff.

[3] *Republic*, 588 C.

CERBERUS IN CLASSIC ART.

Classic art has taken up Cerberus very generously; his treatment, however, is far from being as definite as that of the Greek and Roman poets. Statues, sarcophagi, and vase paintings whose theme is Hades, or scenes laid in Hades, represent him as a ferocious Greek collie, often encircled with serpents, and with a serpent for a tail, but there is no certainty as to the number of his heads. Often he is three-headed in art as in literature, as may be seen conveniently in the reproductions in Baumeister's *Denkmäler des Klassischen Altertums*. Very familiar is the statue in the villa Borghese of Pluto enthroned, three-headed Cerberus by his side.[4] A Greek scarabæus shows a pair of lovers, or a married couple, who have died at the same time, crossing in Charon's ferry. As they are approaching the other bank of the Styx, where a three-headed Cerberus is awaiting them, the girl seems afright and is upheld by her male companion.[5] On the other hand, a bronze in Naples shows the smiling boy Herakles engaged in strangling two serpents, one with each hand. The figure rests on a cylindrical base upon which are depicted eight of the wonderful deeds which Herakles performs later on. By a rope he leads a *two-headed* Cerberus from Hades.[6]

This last of the wonderful deeds of Herakles is a favorite theme of vase pictures. Herakles is regularly accompanied by Hermes and Athena; the dog, whose marvelous shape Homer fails to reveal, is generally two-headed. Such a vase may be seen in Gerhard, *Auserlesene Vasenbilder*, ii. 131.[7] Or still more conveniently, Professor Norton has reproduced[8] an amphora in the Louvre with a picture of the dicephalous Kerberos. Upon the forehead of each of the two heads rises a serpent. Herakles in tunic and lion's skin, armed with bow, quiver, and sword, stoops towards the dog. He holds a chain in his left hand, while he stretches out his right with a petting gesture. Between the two is a tree, against which leans the club of Herakles. Behind him stands Athena.

---

[4] Baumeister, volume I., page 620 (figure 690).

[5] Baumeister, volume I., page 379 (figure 415).

[6] Baumeister, volume I., page 653 (figure 721).

[7] Baumeister, volume I., page 663 (figure 730). See the Frontispiece and its explanation.

[8] *American Journal of Archæology*, volume XI., page 14 (figure 12, page 15).

CERBERUS IN ROMAN
AND MODERN LITERATURE.

Neither Greek literature, nor Greek art, however, really seems to fix either the shape or nature of Kerberos; it was left to the Roman poets to say the last word about him. They finally settle the number of his heads, or the number of his bodies fused in one. He is *triceps* "three-headed," *triplex* or *tergeminus* "threefold," *triformis* "of three bodies," or simply Tricerberus. Tibullus says explicitly that he has both three heads and three tongues: *cui tres sint linguæ tergeminumque caput.* Virgil, in the *Æneid*, vi. 417, has huge Cerberus barking with triple jaws; his neck bristles with serpents. Ovid in his *Metamorphoses*, x. 21, makes Orpheus, looking for dear Eurydice in Tartarus, declare that he did not go down in order that he might chain the three necks, shaggy with serpents, of the monster begotten of Medusa. His business also is settled for all time; he is the terrible, fearless, and watchful janitor, or guardian (*janitor* or *custos*) of Orcus, the Styx, Lethe, or the black Kingdom.[9] And so he remains for modern poets, as when Dante, reproducing Virgil, describes him:[10]

> "When Cerberus, that great worm, had seen us
> His mouth he opened and his fangs were shown,
> And then my leader with his folded palms
> Took of the earth, and filling full his hand,
> Into those hungry gullets flung it down."

Or Shakespeare, *Love's Labor Lost*, v. ii: "Great Hercules is presented by this imp whose club killed Cerberus, the three-headed *canis*."

---

[9] *Custos opaci pervigil regni canis.* Seneca.
[10] *Inferno*, Canto vi., 13 ff.

CLASSICAL EXPLANATIONS OF CERBERUS.

Such classical explanations of Cerberus' shape as I have seen are feeble and foolishly reasonable. Heraclitus, Περὶ ἀπίστων 331, states that Kerberos had two pups. They always attended their father, and therefore he appeared to be three-headed. The mythographer Palaephatos(39) states that Kerberos was considered three-headed from his name Τρικάρηνος which he obtained from the city Trikarenos in Phliasia. And a late Roman rationalistic mythographer by the name of Fulgentius[11] tells us that Petronius defined Cerberus as the lawyer of Hades, apparently because of his three jaws, or the cumulative glibness of three tongues. Fulgentius himself has a *fabula* in which he says that Cerberus means *Creaboros*, that is, "flesh-eating," and that the three heads of Cerberus are respectively, infancy, youth, and old age, through which death has entered the circle of the earth— *per quas introivit mors in orbem terrarum.*[12]

---

[11] See p. 99 of the Teubner edition of his writings.
[12] Fulgentius, Liber I., Fabula VI., de Tricerbero, p. 20 of the Teubner edition.

A MODERN VIEW.

"Lasciate ogni speranza voi ch' entrate"

Can we bid this *"schwankende Gestalt,"* this monstrous vision, floating about upon the filmy photographs of murky Hades, stand still, emerge into light, and assume clear and reasonable outlines?

> "Hence loathed melancholy of Cerberus and blackest Midnight born."

An American humorist, John Kendrick Bangs, who likes to place his skits in Hades, steps in "where angels fear to tread," and launches with a light heart the discussion as to whether Cerberus is one or more dogs. The city of Cimmeria in Hades, having tried asphalt pavement, which was found too sloppy for that climate, and Nicholson wood pavement, which kept taking fire, decides on Belgian blocks. In order to meet the new expense a dog-tax is imposed. Since Cerberus belongs to Hades as a whole, the state must pay his tax, and is willing enough to do so—on Cerberus as one dog. The city, however, endeavors to collect on three dogs—one license for each head. Two infernal coppers, sent to impound Cerberus, fare not well, one of them being badly chewed up by Cerberus, the other nabbed bodily and thrown into the Styx. In consequence of this they obtain damages from the city. The city then decides to bring suit against the state. The bench consists of Apollyon himself and Judge Blackstone; Coke appears for the city, Catiline for the state. The first dog-catcher, called to testify, and asked whether he is familiar with dogs, replies in the affirmative, adding that he had never got quite so intimate with one as he got with him.

"With whom?" asks Coke.

"Cerberus," replies the witness.

"Do you consider him to be one dog, two dogs, or three dogs?"

Catiline objects to this question as a leading one, but Coke manages to get it in under another form: "How many dogs did you see when you saw Cerberus?"

"Three, anyhow," replies the witness with feeling, "though afterwards I thought there was a whole bench-show atop of me."

On cross-examination Catiline asks him blandly: "My poor friend, if you considered Cerberus to be three dogs anyhow, why did you in your examination a moment since refer to the avalanche of caninity, of which you so affectingly speak, as him?"

"He is a him," sturdily says the witness. After this Coke, discomfited, decides to call his second witness: "What is your business?" asks Coke, after the usual preliminaries.

"I'm out of business. Livin' on my damages."

"What damages?"

"Them I got from the city for injuries did me by that there—I should say them there—dorgs, Cerberus."

And so on. Catiline gains the day for the state by his superior logic; the city of Cimmeria must content itself with taxes on a single dog. But the logic of the facts, it will appear, are with the dog-catchers, Judge Coke, and the city of Cimmeria as against the state of Hades: Cerberus is more than one dog.

FUTURE LIFE IN THE VEDA.

India is the home of the Cerberus myth in its clearest and fullest development. In order to appreciate its nature we must bear in mind that the early Hindu conceptions of a future life are auspicious, and quite the reverse of sombre. The statements in the Veda about life after death exclude all notions of hell. The early visions are simple, poetic and cheerful. The bodies of the dead are burned and their ashes are consigned to earth. But this is viewed merely as a symbolic act of preparation—cooking it is called forthright—for another life of joy. The righteous forefathers of old who died before, they have found another good place. Especially Yama, the first mortal, has gone to the great rivers on high; he has searched out, like a pioneer, the way for all his descendants: "He went before and found a dwelling which no power can debar us from. Our fathers of old have traveled the path; it leads every earth-born mortal thither. There in the midst of the highest heaven beams unfading light and eternal waters flow; there every wish is fulfilled on the rich meadows of Yama." Day by day Yama sends forth two dogs, his messengers, to search out among men those who are to join the fathers that are having an excellent time in Yama's company.

THE TWO DOGS OF YAMA.

The tenth book of the *Rig-Veda* contains in hymns 14-18 a collection of funeral stanzas quite unrivaled for mythological and ethnological interest in the literature of ancient peoples. In hymn 14 there are three stanzas (10-12) that deal with the two dogs of Yama. This is the classical passage, all depends upon its interpretation. They contain detached statements which take up the idea from different points of view, that are not easily harmonized as long as the dogs are merely ordinary canines; they resolve themselves fitly and neatly into a pair of natural objects, if we follow closely all the ideas which the Hindus associated with them.

In the first place, it is clear that we are dealing with the conception of Cerberus. In stanza 10 the two dogs are conceived as ill-disposed creatures, standing guard to keep the departed souls out of bliss. The soul on its way to heaven is addressed as follows:

"Run past straightway the two four-eyed dogs, the spotted and (the dark), the brood of Saramā; enter in among the propitious fathers who hold high feast with Yama."

A somewhat later text, the book of house-rite of Āçvalāyana, has the notion of the sop to Cerberus: "To the two dogs born in the house of (Yama) Vivasvant's son, to the dark and the spotted, I have given a cake; do ye guard me ever on my road!"

The twelfth stanza of the *Rig-Veda* hymn strikes a somewhat different note which suggests both good and evil in the character of the two dogs: "The two brown, broad-nosed messengers of Yama, life-robbing, wander among men. May they restore to us to-day the auspicious breath of life, that we may behold the sun." Evidently the part of the Cerberi here is not in harmony with their function in stanza 10: instead of debarring men from the abodes of bliss they pick out the dead that are ultimately destined to boon companionship with Yama. The same idea is expressed simply and clearly in prayers for long life in the *Atharva-Veda*: "The two dogs of Yama, the dark and the spotted, that guard the road (to heaven), that have been dispatched, shall not (go after) thee! Come hither, do not long to be away! Do not tarry here with thy mind turned to a distance." (viii. 1. 9.) And again: "Remain here, O man, with thy soul entire! Do not follow the two messengers of Yama; come to the abodes of the living." (v. 30. 6.)

These prayers contain the natural, yet under the circumstances rather paradoxical, desire to live yet a little longer upon the earth in the light of the sun.

Fitfully the mortal Hindu regales himself with saccharine promises of paradise; in his every-day mood he clings to life and shrinks with the uneasy sense that his paradise may not materialize, even if the hope is expressed glibly and fluently. The real craving is expressed in numberless passages: "May we live a hundred autumns, surrounded by lusty sons." Homer's Hades has wiped out this inconsistency, only to substitute another. Odysseus, on returning from his visit to Hades, exclaims baldly: "Better a swineherd on the surface of the earth in the light of the sun than king of the shades in Hades." It is almost adding insult to injury to have the road to such a Hades barred by Cerberus. This latter paradox must be removed in order that the myth shall become intelligible.

The eleventh of the *Rig-Veda* stanzas presents the two dogs as guides of the soul ψυχοπόμποι to heaven: "To thy two four-eyed, road-guarding, man-beholding watch-dogs entrust him, O King Yama, and bestow on him prosperity and health."

THE TWO DOGS IN HEAVEN.

With the change of the abode of the dead from inferno to heaven the two Cerberi are *eo ipso* also evicted. That follows of itself, even if we had not explicit testimony. A legend of the Brāhmana-texts, the Hindu equivalent of the Talmud, tells repeatedly that there are two dogs *in heaven*, and that these two dogs are Yama's dogs. I shall present two versions of the story, a kind of Γιγαντομαχία in order to establish the equation between the terms "two dogs of Yama," and "two heavenly dogs."

There were Asuras (demons) named Kālakānjas. They piled up a fire altar in order to obtain the world of heaven. Man by man they placed a brick upon it. The god Indra, passing himself off for a Brahmin, put on a brick for himself. They climbed up to heaven. Indra pulled out his brick; they tumbled down. And they who tumbled down became spiders; two flew up, and became the two heavenly dogs." (Brāhmana of the *Tāittirīyas* 1. 1. 2.)

"The Asuras (demons) called Kālakānjas piled bricks for an altar, saying: 'We will ascend to heaven.' Indra, passing himself off for a Brahmin, came to them; he put on a brick. They at first came near getting to heaven; then Indra tore out his brick. The Asuras becoming quite feeble fell down; the two that were uppermost became the dogs of Yama, those which were lower became spiders." (Brāhmana of the *Māitra* 1. 6. 9.)

This theme is so well fixed in the minds of the time that it is elaborated in a charm to preserve from some kind of injury, addressed to the mythic figures of the legend:

"Through the air he flies looking down upon all beings: with the majesty of the heavenly dog, with that oblation would we pay homage to thee.

"The three Kālakānjas, that are fixed upon the sky like gods, all these I have called to help, to render this person free from harm.

"In the waters is thy origin, upon the heavens thy home, in the middle of the sea, and upon the earth, thy greatness; with the majesty of the heavenly dog, with that oblation would we pay homage to thee." (*Atharva-Veda* vi., 80.)

The single heavenly dog that is described here is of no mean interest. The passage proves the individual character of each of the two dogs of Yama; they cannot be a vague pair of heavenly dogs, but must be based each upon some definite phenomenon in the heavens.

Yet another text, Hiranyakeçin's book of house-rites, locates the dogs of Yama, describing them in unmistakable language, in heaven: "The brood of Saramā, dark beneath and brown, run, looking down upon the sea." (ii. 7. 2.)

THE TWO DOGS OF YAMA
EXPLAIN THEMSELVES.

There are not many things in heaven that can be represented as a pair, coursing across the sky, looking down upon the sea, and having other related properties. My readers will make a shrewd guess, but I prefer to let the texts themselves unfold the transparent mystery. The Veda of the *Katha* school (xxxvii. 14) says: "These two dogs of Yama, verily, are day and night," and the Brāhmana of the *Kāushītak-ins* (ii. 9) argues in Talmudic strain: "At eve, when the sun has gone down, before darkness has set in, one should sacrifice the *agnihotra*-sacrifice; in the morning before sunrise, when darkness is dispelled, at that time, one should sacrifice the *agnihotra*-sacrifice; at that time the gods arrive. Therefore (the two dogs of Yama) Çyāma and Çabala (the dark and the spotted) tear to pieces the *agnihotra* of him that sacrifices otherwise. Çabala is the day; Çyāma is the night. He who sacrifices in the night, his *agnihotra* Çyāma tears asunder; he who sacrifices in broad day-light, his *agnihotra* Çabala tears asunder." Even more drily the two dogs of Yama are correlated with the time-markers of heaven in a passage of the *Tāittirīya-Veda* (v. 7. 19); here sundry parts of the sacrificial horse are assigned to four cosmic phe-nomena in the following order: 1. Sun and moon. 2. Çyāma and Çabala (the two dogs of Yama). 3. Dawn. 4. Evening twilight. So that the dogs of Yama are sand-wiched in between sun and moon on the one side, dawn and evening twilight on the other. Obviously they are here, either as a special designation of day and night, or their physical equivalents, sun and moon. And now the *Çatapatha-Brāhmana* says explicitly: "The moon verily is the divine dog; he looks down upon the cattle of the sacrificer." And again a passage in the Kashmir version of the *Atharva-Veda* says: "The four-eyed dog (the moon) surveys by night the sphere of the night."

SUN AND MOON AS STATIONS ON THE WAY TO SALVATION.

Even the theosophic Upanishads are compelled to make their way through this tolerably crude mythology when they come to deal with the passage of the soul to release from existence and absorption in the universal Brahma. The human mind does not easily escape some kind of eschatological topography. The Brahma itself may be devoid of all properties, universal, pervasive, situated below as well as above, the one true thing everywhere; still even the Upanishads finally fix upon a world of Brahma, and that is above, not below, nor elsewhere; hence the soul must pass the great cosmic potencies that seem to lie on the road from the sublunary regions to Brahma. The *Kāushītaki Upanishad* (1. 2. 3) arranges that all who leave this world first go to the moon, the moon being the door of the world of light. The moon asks certain theosophic questions; he alone who can answer them is considered sufficiently emancipated to advance to the world of Brahma. He who cannot—alas!—is born again as worm or as fly; as fish or as fowl; as lion or as boar; as bull or tiger or man; or as something else—any old thing, as we should say—in this place or in that place, according to the quality of his works and the degree of his knowledge; that is, in accordance with the doctrine of *Karma*. Similarly the *Māitri Upanishad* (vi. 38) sketches salvation as follows: When a mortal no longer approves of wrath, and ponders the true wish, he penetrates the veil that encloses the Brahma, breaks through the concentric circles of sun, moon, fire, etc., that occupy the ether. Only then does he behold the supreme thing that is founded upon its own greatness only. And now the *Chāndogya Upanishad* (viii. 13) has the same idea, mentioning both moon and sun by their ancient names and in their capacity as dogs of Yama. The soul of the aspirant for fusion with Brahma resorts purgatorio-fashion alternately to Çyāma (the moon-dog) and Çabala (the sun-dog): "From Çyāma (the moon) do I resort to Çabala (the sun); from Çabala to Çyāma. Shaking off sin, as a steed shakes off (the loose hair of) its mane, as the moon frees itself from the maw of Rāhu, the demon of eclipse, casting aside my body, my real self delivered, do I enter into the uncreated world of Brahma."[13]

---

[13] Both Çankara, the great Hindu theologian and commentator of the Upanishads, as well as all modern interpreters of the Upanishads, have failed to see the sense of this passage.

ANALYSIS OF THE MYTH.

Hindu mythology is famous for what I should like to hear called arrested personification, or arrested anthropomorphism. More than elsewhere mythic figures seem here to cling to the dear memories of their birth and youth. This is due in part to the unequaled impressiveness of nature in India; in part to the dogged schematism of the Hindu mind, which dislikes to let go of any part of a thing from the beginning to end. On the one hand, their constant, almost too rhythmic resort to nature in their poetry, and on the other, their Vedānta philosophy, or for that matter their *Ars amatoria* (*Kāmaçāstra*), the latter worked out with painstaking and undignified detail, illustrate the two points. Hence we find here a situation which is familiar enough in the Veda, but scarcely and rarely exhibited in other mythological fields. Dogs, the two dogs of Yama are, but yet, too, sun and moon. It is quite surprising how well the attributes of things so different keep on fitting them both well enough. The color and brightness of the sun jumps with the fixed epithet, "spotted," of the sun-dog Çabala; the moon-dog is black (Çyāma or Çyāva). Sun and moon, as they move across the sky, are the natural messengers of Yama, seated on high in the abode of the blessed, but Yama is after all death, and death hounds us all. Epithets like "man-beholding," or "guarding the way," suit neutrally both conceptions. Above all, the earliest statements about Yama's dogs are relieved of their inconsistencies. On the one hand the exhortation to the dead to run past the two dogs in order to get to heaven, suits the idea of the heavenly dogs who are coursing across the sky. On the other hand, by an easy, though quite contrary, change of mental position, the same two heavenly dogs are the guides who guard the way and look upon men favorably; hence they are ordered by Yama to take charge of the dead and to furnish them such health and prosperity as the shades happen to have use for. Again, by an equally simple shift of position, sun and moon move among men as the messengers of death; by night and by day men perish, while these heavenly bodies alternate in their presence among men."[14] Hence a text of the Veda can say in a similar mood: "May Day and Night procure for us long life" (House-book of Āçvalāyana, ii. 4. 14). Conversely it is a commonplace of the Veda to say that day and night destroy the lives of men. One text says that, "day and night are the encircling arms of death" (Brāhmana of the *Kāushītakin*, ii. 9). Another, more explicitly, "the year is death; by means of day and night does it destroy the life of mortals (*Çatapatha-Brāhmana*, x. 4. 3. 1). He who wishes to be released from the grim grip of day and night sacrifices (symbolically)

[14] Cf. the notion of the sun as the "highest death" in *Tāittirīva Brāhmana*, 1. 8. 4.

white and black rice, and pronounces the words: "Hail to Day; hail to Night; hail to Release" (Brāhmana of the *Tāittiriya*, iii. 1. 6. 2). Who does not remember in this connection the parable widely current in the Orient, in which two rats, one white, the other black, gnaw alternately, but without let-up, the plant or tree of life?[15]

---

[15] See Ernst Kuhn, Festgruss an Otto von Böhtlingk, page 68 ff.

THE CERBERI IN THE NORSE MYTH.

Norse mythology also contains certain animal pairs which seem to reflect the two dualities, sun and moon, and day and night. There is here no certainty as to detail; the Norse myth is advanced and congealed, if not spurious, as Professor Bugge and his school would have us believe. At the feet of Odin lie his two wolves, Geri and Freki, "Greedy" and "Voracious." They hurl themselves across the lands when peace is broken. Who shall say that they are to be entirely dissociated from Yama's two dogs of death? The virgin Menglödh sleeps in her wonderful castle on the mountain called Hyfja, guarded by the two dogs Geri and Gifr, "Greedy" and "Violent," who take turns in watching; only alternately may they sleep as they watch the Hyfja mountain. "One sleeps by night, the other by day, and thus no one may enter" (*Fiölsvinnsmâl*, 16). It is not necessary to suppose any direct connection between this fable and the Vedic myth, but the root of the thought, no matter from how great a distance it may have come, and how completely it may have been worked over by the Norse skald, is, after all, alternating sun and moon and their partners, day and night.

CERBERUS IN THE PERSIAN AVESTA.

No reasonable student of mythology will demand of a myth so clearly destined for fructification an everlasting virginal inviolateness. From the start almost the two dogs of Yama are the brood of Saramā. Why? Saramā is the female messenger of the gods, at the root identical with Hermes or Hermeias; she is therefore the predestined mother of those other messengers, the two four-eyed dogs of Yama. And as the latter are her litter the myth becomes retroactive; she herself is fancied later on as a four-eyed bitch (*Atharva-Veda*, iv. 20. 7). Similarly the epithet "broad-nosed" stands not in need of mythic interpretation, as soon as it has become a question of life-hunting dogs. Elusive and vague, I confess, is the persistent and important attribute "four-eyed." This touch is both old and widespread. The *Avesta*, the bible of the ancient Iranians, has reduced the Cerberus myth to stunted rudiments. In *Vendidad*, xiii. 8. 9, the killing of dogs is forbidden, because the soul of the slayer "when passing to the other world, shall fly amid louder howling and fiercer pursuit than the sheep does when the wolf rushes upon it in the lofty forest. No soul will come and meet his departing soul and help it through the howls and pursuit in the other world; nor will the dogs that keep the Cinvad bridge (the bridge to paradise) help his departing soul through the howls and pursuit in the other world." The *Avesta* also conceives this dog to be four-eyed. When a man dies, as soon as the soul has parted from the body, the evil one, the corpse-devil (Druj Nasu), from the regions of hell, falls upon the dead. Whoever henceforth touches the corpse becomes unclean, and makes unclean whomsoever he touches. The devil is expelled from the dead by means of the "look of the dog": a "four-eyed dog" is brought near the body and is made to look at the dead; as soon as he has done so the devil flees back to hell (*Vendidad*, vii. 7; viii. 41). It is not easy to fetch from a mythological hell mythological monsters for casual purposes, especially as men are always engaged in dying upon the earth. Herakles is the only one who, one single time, performed this notable "stunt." So the Parsis, being at a loss to find four-eyed dogs, interpret the name as meaning a dog with two spots over the eyes. Curiously enough the Hindu scholiasts also regularly interpret the term "four-eyed" in exactly the same way, "with spots over the eyes." And the Vedic ritual in its turn has occasion to realize the mythological four-eyed dog in practice. The horse, at the horse-sacrifice, must take a bath for consecration to the holy end to which it is put. It must also be guarded against hostile influences. A low-caste man brings a four-eyed dog—here obviously the symbol of the hostile powers— kills him with a club, and afterwards places him under the feet of the horse. It is scarcely necessary to state that this is a dog with spots over his eyes, and that he is a symbol of Cerberus.[16]

---

[16] Similar notions in Russia and Russian Asia are reported by Wsevolod Miller, Atti del iv. *Congresso Internazionale degli Orientalisti*, vol. ii. p. 43; and by Casartelli, *Babylonian and Oriental Record*, iv. 266 ff. They are most likely derived from Iranian sources.

THE TERM "FOUR-EYED."

The epithet "four-eyed" may possibly contain a tentative coagulation of the two dogs in one. The capacity of the two dogs to see both by day (the sun) and by night (the moon) may have given the myth a slight start into the direction of the two-headed Greek Cerberus. But there is the alternate possibility that four-eyed is but a figure of speech for "sharp-sighted," especially as I have shown elsewhere that the parallel expression "to run with four feet" is a Vedic figure of speech for "swift of foot."[17] Certainly the god Agni, "Fire," is once in the *Rig-Veda* (i. 31. 13) called "four-eyed," which can only mean "sharp-sighted."

---

[17] See *American Journal of Philology*, vol. XI., p. 355.

THE DUAL ÇABALĀU.

The two dogs of Yama derive their proper names from their color epithets. The passages above make it clear that Çyāma (rarely Çyāva), "the black," is the moon dog, and that Çabala, "the spotted, or brindled," is the sun dog. In one early passage (*Rig-Veda*, x. 14. 10) both dogs are named in the dual as Çabalāu. But for a certain Vedic usage one might think that "the two spotted ones" was their earliest designation. The usage referred to is the eliptic dual: a close or natural pair, each member of which suggests the other, may be expressed through the dual of one of them, as when either *mātarāu* or *pitarāu*, literally, "the two mothers," and "the two fathers," each mean "the two parents."[18] From this we may conclude that Çabalāu means really Çabala and Çyāma, and not the two Çabalas, that is, "the two spotted ones."

---

[18] Similarly in Greek **Αἴαντε** means Ajax and Teukros; see Delbrück, *Vergleichende Syntax*, i. 137.

IS ÇABALAS = Κέρβερος?

More than a hundred years ago the Anglo-Indian Wilford, in the *Asiatick Researches*, iii., page 409, wrote: "Yama, the regent of hell, has two dogs, according to the Purānas; one of them named Cerbura, or varied; the other Syama, or black." He then compares Cerbura with Kerberos, of course. The form Cerbura he obtained from his consulting Pandit, who explained the name Çabala by the Sanskrit word *karbura* "variegated," a regular gloss of the Hindu scholiasts.

About fifty years later a number of distinguished scholars of the past generation, Max Müller, Albrecht Weber, and Theodor Benfey, compared the word Çabala with Greek **Κέρβερος** (rarely **Κέρβελος**), but, since then, this identification has been assailed in numerous quarters with some degree of heat, because it suffers from a slight phonetic difficulty. One need but remember the swift changes which the name of Apollo passes through in the mouths of the Greeks— Απόλλων, Απέλλων, Αππέλλων, Απείλων, Απλουν[19]—to realize that it is useless to demand strict phonetic conservation of mythic proper names. The nominative Çabalas, translated sound for sound into Greek, yields **Κεβερος, Κεβελος**; *vice versa*, **Κέβρερος**? translated sound for sound into Vedic Sanskrit yields Çalbalas, or perhaps, dialectically, Çabbalas. It is a sober view that considers it rather surprising that the two languages have not manipulated their respective versions of the word so as to increase still further the phonetic distance between them. Certainly the burden is now to prove that the identification is to be rejected, and, I think, that the soundest linguistic science will refuse ultimately to consider the phonetic discrepancy between the two words as a matter of serious import.

But whether the names Çabalas and Kerberos are identical or not, the myth itself is the thing. The explanation which we have coaxed step by step from the texts of the Veda imparts to the myth a definite character: it is no longer a dark and uncertain touch in the troubled visions of hell, but an uncommonly lucid treatment of an important cosmic phenomenon. Sun and moon course across the sky: beyond is the abode of light and the blessed. The coursers are at one moment regarded as barring the way to heaven; at another as outposts who may guide the soul to heaven. In yet another mood, as they constantly, day by day, look down upon the race of men, dying day by day, they are regarded as picking daily candidates for the final journey. In due time Yama and his heaven are degraded to a mere Pluto and hell; then the terrible character of the two dogs is all that can be left to them.

---

[19] See Usener, Götternamen, p. 303 ff.

And the two dogs blend into a unit variously, either a four-eyed Parsi dog, or a two-headed—finally a plural-headed—Kerberos.

OTHER DOGS OF HELL.

The peace of mind of one or the other reader is likely to be disturbed by the appearance of a hell-dog here and there among peoples outside of the Indo-European (Aryan) family. So, e. g., I. G. Müller, in his *Geschichte der Americanischen Urreligionen*, second edition, p. 88, mentions a dog who threatens to swallow the souls in their passage of the river of hell. There was a custom among the Mordwines to put a club into the coffin with the corpse, to enable him to drive away the watch-dogs at the gate of the nether world.[20] The Mordwines, however, have borrowed much of their mythology from the Iranians. The Hurons and Iroquois told the early missionaries that after death the soul must cross a deep and swift river on a bridge formed by a single slender tree, where it had to defend itself against the attacks of a dog.[21] No sane ethnologist or philologer will insist that all these conceptions are related *genetically*, that there is nothing accidental in the repetition of the idea. The dog is prominent in animal mythology; one of his functions is to watch. It is quite possible, nay likely, that a dog, pure and simple, has strayed occasionally into this sphere of conceptions without any further organic meaning—simply as a baying, hostile watch-dog. But we cannot prove anything by an ignorant *non possumus;* the conception *may*, even if we cannot say *must*, after all in each case, have been derived from essentially the same source: the dead journeying upward to heaven interfered with by a coursing heavenly body, the sun or the moon, or both. Anyhow, the organic quality of the Indo-European, or at least the Hindu myth makes it guide and philosopher. From dual sun and moon coursing across the sky to the two hell-hounds, each step of development is no less clear than from Zeus pater, "Father Sky," to breezy Jove, the gentleman about town with his escapades and amours. To reverse the process, to imagine that the Hindus started with two visionary dogs and finally identified them with sun and moon—that is as easy and natural as it is for a river to flow up the hill back to its source.

---

[20] Max Müller, *Contributions to the Science of Mythology*, p. 240.
[21] Brinton, *The Myths of the New World*. Second Edition, p. 265.

MAX MÜLLER'S CERBERUS.

The rudiment of the present essay in Comparative Mythology was published by the writer some years ago in a learned journal, under the title, "The two dogs of Yama in a new role."[22] My late lamented friend, Max Müller, the gifted writer who knew best of all men how to rivet the attention of the cultivated public upon questions of this sort, did me the honor to notice my proposition in an article in the *London Academy* of August 13, 1892 (number 1058, page 134-5), entitled "Professor Bloomfield's Contributions to the Interpretation of the Veda." In this article he seems to try to establish a certain similarity between his conception of the Kerberos myth and my own. This similarity seems to me to be entirely illusory. Professor Müller's own last words on the subject in the Preface of his *Contributions to the Science of Mythology* (p. xvi.), will make clear the difference between our views. He identifies, as he always has identified, Kerberos with the Vedic stem *çarvara*, from which is derived *çarvarī*, "night." To quote his own words: "The germ of the idea ... must be discovered in that nocturnal darkness, that *çārvaram tamas*, which native mythologists in India had not yet quite forgotten in post-Vedic times." With such a view my own has not the least point of contact. Çabala, the name of one of the dogs, means "spotted, bright"; it is the name of the sun-dog; it is quite the opposite of the *çārvaram tamas*. The name of the moon-dog, and, by transfer, the dog of the night, is Çyāma or Çyāva "black," not Çabala, nor Çarvara. The association of the two dogs with day and night is the association of sun and moon with their respective diurnal divisions, and nothing more. Of Cimmerian gloom there can be nothing in the myth primarily, because it deals at the beginning with heaven, and not with hell; with an auspicious, and not a gloomy, vision of life after death.

---

[22] Presented to the American Oriental Society at its meeting May 5, 1891; and printed in its Journal, Vol. XV., pp. 163 ff.

CERBERUS AND COMPARATIVE MYTHOLOGY.

In conclusion I would draw the attention of those scholars, writers, and publicists that have declared bankruptcy against the methods and results of Comparative Mythology to the present attempt to establish an Indo-European naturalistic myth. I would ask them to consider, in the light of the Veda, that it is probable that the early notions of future life turn to the visible heaven with its sun and moon, rather than to the topographically unstable and elusive caves and gullies that lead to a wide-gated Hades. In heaven, therefore, and not in hell, is the likely breeding spot of the Cerberus myth. On the way to heaven there is but one pair that can have shaped itself reasonably in the minds of primitive observers into a pair of Cerberi. Sun and moon, the Veda declares, are the Cerberi. In due time, and by gradual stages, the heaven myth became a hell myth. The Vedic seers had no Pluto, no Hades, no Styx, and no Charon; yet they had the pair of dogs. Now when Yama and his heaven become Pluto and hell, then, and only then, Yama's dogs are on a plane with the three-headed, or two-headed, Greek Kerberos. Is it not likely that the chthonic hell visions of the Greeks were also preceded by heavenly visions, and that Kerberos originally sprang from heaven? Consider, too, the breadth and the persistence of these ideas, their simple background, and their natural transition from one feature to another in the myth of Cerberus; that is, the notions of sun and moon (day and night) in their relation to the precarious life of man upon the earth, his death, and his future life. For my part, I do not believe that the honest critics of the methods and results of Comparative Mythology, though they have been made justly suspicious by the many failures in this field, will ever successfully "run past, straightway, the two four-eyed dogs, the spotted and the dark, the Çabalāu, the brood of Saramā."

Lector House believes that a society develops through a two-fold approach of continuous learning and adaptation, which is derived from the study of classic literary works spread across the historic timeline of literature records. Therefore, we aim at reviving, repairing and redeveloping all those inaccessible or damaged but historically as well as culturally important literature across subjects so that the future generations may have an opportunity to study and learn from past works to embark upon a journey of creating a better future.

This book is a result of an effort made by Lector House towards making a contribution to the preservation and repair of original ancient works which might hold historical significance to the approach of continuous learning across subjects.

HAPPY READING & LEARNING!

LECTOR HOUSE LLP
E-MAIL: info@lectorhouse.com